Purple Ronnie's

Guide to

THE OPPOSITE SEX

♡

by Purple Ronnie

Purple Ronnie's Little Guide to Men first published 2000 by Boxtree
Purple Ronnie's Little Guide to Girls first published 2000 by Boxtree
Purple Ronnie's Little Guide to Boyfriends first published 1999 by Boxtree
Purple Ronnie's Little Poems for Friends first published 1999 by Boxtree
This omnibus edition published 2003 for Index by Boxtree
an imprint of PanMacmillan Publishers Ltd.
20 New Wharf Road
London N1 9RR

www.macmillan.com

Associated companies throughout the world

ISBN 0 7522 2506 5

9 8 7 6 5 4 3 2 1

A CIP catalogue record for this book is
available from the British Library

Text by Giles Andreae
Illustrations by Janet Cronin
Printed and Bound by Bath Press

☆ MEN

GIRLS ✿

☆ Boyfriends

FRIENDS ✿

MEN

☆

a man →
Flurb

Arty Men

floaty hair →

posy chin fluff

girly shirt

Deep Poems

An Arty Man's brain is on a completely different planet to everyone else's

sproing

cuckoo cuckoo

a poem about
Arty Men

Arty Men like to be different
To show how creative they are
So don't be surprised
If they butter their thighs
And start barking out loud at
                    your car

wow!
he's so
creative

wag

woof

Macho Men

Sometimes it can be difficult to find a Macho Man's doodah because there are so many muscles in the way

Macho Men

Some men think it's cool to bare
A bulging chest with loads of hair
But if you talk to one you'll find
His brains are stuck up his
                              behind

Mummy's Boys

nice parting

chubby cheeks

favourite teddy

Mummy's Sarnies

clean pants

Mummy's Boys' clothes are incredibly tidy, they have creases in everything and they always smell of roses

Special pyjamas

night night

Mummy's Boys

When you date a Mummy's Boy
They always bring their mums
Then sit there cuddling their shawls
And sucking on their thumbs

Lager Lads

A Lager Lad's favourite joke is showing his bottom to people

a poem about
Lager Lads

Lager Lads love going out with
their mates

In fact it's their favourite trick

To gobble down masses of curry
and beer

And pass out in piles of sick

Weeds

Grown-up Weeds have two straggly hairs on their chests which they are very proud of

a poem about
↓
Weeds

Some men think weeds are
pathetic
Because they're so fussy and neat
But most people find
That they're friendly and kind
And girls always say that they're
sweet

Wide Boys

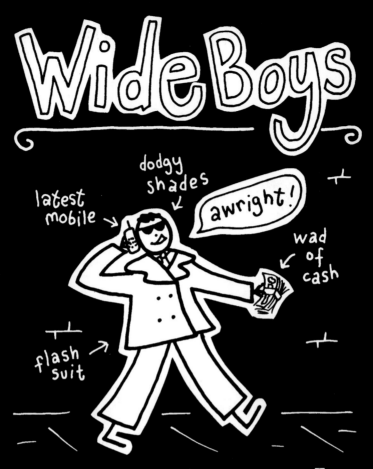

A Wide Boy will love you forever if you let him Do It with you in the back of his car

a poem about

Wide Boys

They're always on their mobile
phones
Cutting dodgy deals
Looking sharp in shiny suits
And nifty sets of wheels

I'll do the fluffy bears
at twenty quid and
the wind-up grannies
at fifty

speed

Girly Men

Girly Men's bathrooms are stuffed full of all sorts of lotions and potions for making themselves feel gorgeous

a poem about
Girly Men

Girly Men think playing sport is
too rough
So they love to go shopping instead
And when they get home
They spend hours on the phone
Before wearing their face masks
to bed

Slobs

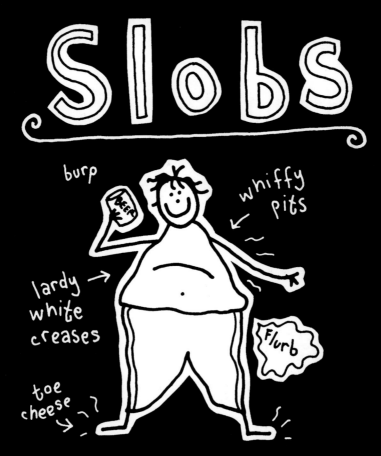

A Slob's favourite kind of date is to have a cosy dinner for two at home

a poem about
Slobs

They walk around in clouds of smoke
They splutter burp and wheeze
They live off mouldy sausages
And whiff of rancid cheese

a poem about a
Sport↓ Man

No girl can get close to a
                    Sport Man

Without passing out on the spot
The air in his room
Has the subtle perfume
Of the sweat on a wrestler's bot

Gadget Men

Gadget Men speak in a language that only other Gadget Men can understand

a poem about
↓
Gadget Men

A Gadget Man will never be
The lover of your dreams
Cos the only things that turn
them on
Are groovy new machines

Perfect Man

gorgeous smile

great sense of humour

cute bum

Perfect Men know exactly where to touch you and they can keep going all night long

rummage

o o ooh
a ahh

a poem about a

Perfect Man

Most girls want a man who is perfect
But maybe not many exist
Who've got charm and panache
Several sackloads of cash
And a willy the size of your wrist

GIRLS

a girl →

Girly Girls

There is nothing a Girly Girl loves more than watching a good weepy movie on the telly

a poem about
Girly Girls

Girly girls are lovely
 But one snog might be enough
Cos their lips are made of sugar
But their brains are made of fluff

Hippy Chicks

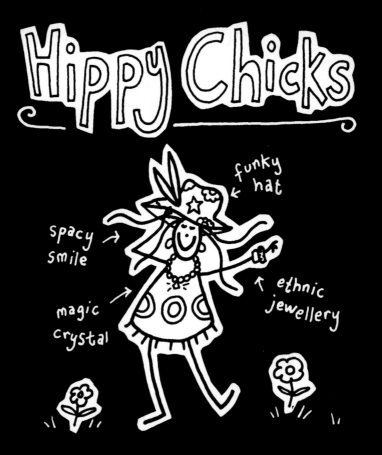

The moon always makes Hippy Chicks feel incredibly sexy

a poem about

Hippy Chicks

They paint their nails with love hearts

And put flowers on their cars

And they like to boogie naked

Underneath the stars

Posh Girls

When it comes to Doing It Posh Girls can sometimes have rather strange fantasies

a poem about
Posh Girls

No matter where they come from
They always talk the same
And they like to give each other
A very silly name

Sex Goddesses

saucy smile

skimpy dress

wiggle

pert bum

sizzle

Sex Goddesses often try to talk about brainy things in case you only fancy them for their looks

...so how can we prove that we really exist at all?

...er good point ...um

a poem about ↓

Sex Goddesses

They pout at themselves in the mirror
To get into Sex Goddess mode
Then wink at the boys who walk past them
And smile as their trousers explode

Earth Mothers

Earth Mothers do not need jobs because they can grow everything they need at home

a poem about
Earth Mothers

They love having baths in rhinoceros
                                    dung
And rubbing their bosoms with clay
It may not look pretty
 Or smell very nice
But it's just much more natural
                            that way

Ladettes

Ladettes believe in Girl Power, and they think most men are boring

a poem about
Ladettes

Dating Ladettes is quite frightening

Because they are easily able

To gobble hot curries

Drink twenty-five pints

And then nail your knob to the table

Fashion Girls

cool shades →

← trendy mobile

big boots ↓

↗ teeny handbag

Fashion Girls get very concerned about things that no-one else would ever notice

that's so last season!

style crime!

wrong trainers ↓

a poem about
↓
Fashion Girls

If you date a fashion girl
Your social life just stops
Cos you'll be spending every
                         weekend

Being dragged around the shops

Mumsy Girls

sensible hairstyle →

← roomy skirt

big handbag →

sturdy shoes

stride

In private Mumsy Girls love to spank naughty little boys

you little terror!

← Madame spanky

a poem about
Mumsy Girls

It's best to avoid them in public

Cos if you sneak off to the lav

They shout at you "please wipe
your bottom

And don't come back here till you
have"

Sporty Girls

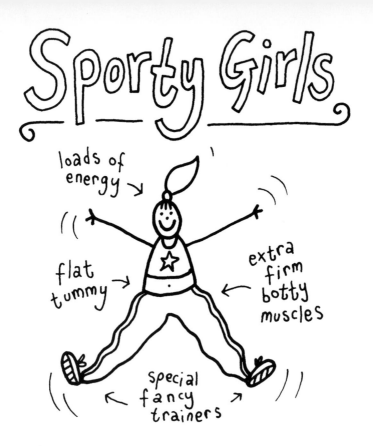

Sporty Girls are so fit that it usually only takes one drink to get them completely pissed

a poem about
Sporty Girls

It's best to tell a Sporty Girl
That she's the one for you
Cos if you don't
She'll grab your wrist
And break you arm in two

Bimbettes

There is nothing a Bimbette loves more than a good night out with the girls

a poem about ↓ Bimbettes

They love to go shopping together

And spend all the money they have

At night they just dance round their handbags

And laugh about boys in the lav

Perfect Girls

thinks
I'm fab

lovely
smile →

↖ sexy
bod

saucy ↗
undies

When you take your clothes off for the
first time a Perfect Girl knows
exactly what to say

you *are* a
big boy!

a poem about

Perfect Girls

You may think I'm being soft-headed
You may think I'm being a fool
But I would call any girl perfect
Who tells me I'm sexy and cool

Boyfriends

a poem for a
Boyfriend

You're a hunky handsome
heart-throb

You're a fab and groovy dude

You're a juicy lump of gorgeousness

A scrumptious plate of food

You're a hot and horny lover

And if I had my way

I would smother you in chocolate

And feast on you all day

a poem about
Letting Off

Some people get lots of pleasure
From books or from music or art
But you seem to think it's
                    fantastic
To just have a really good fart

Warning:-

As soon as your boyfriend knows you love him...

...he will start picking his nose in front of you and farting out loud

Saying I Love You

Boys usually only say
I Love You
When they want to
Do It with you

a poem about
↓
Trousers

Men just don't know how to turn
women on

Though they try to excite and
arouse us

They should be romantic and
caring and kind

But instead they just tear off
their trousers

The Bathroom

Boys make unbelieveable smells
when they go to the lav

"grunt"

whiff

LAV

pong

They always leave the seat up
And they <u>never</u> clean the bath

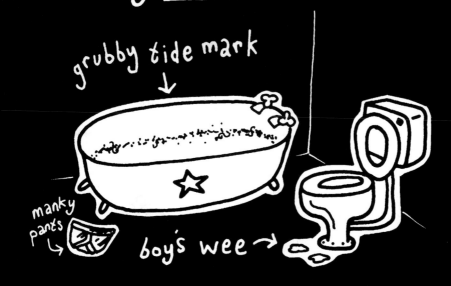

grubby tide mark
↓

manky
pants
↳

boy's wee →

a poem about being
Smelly

You take off your shirt
And your armpits are whiffy
You take off your socks
And your feet are all niffy
You give me a hug
And you're terribly smelly
Then you ask me to kiss you
- NOT ON YOUR NELLIE!

Cuddling

Most boyfriends do not understand the point of cuddling...

...it is best to explain it to them gently

a poem about

Cuddling

I sometimes have feelings
You don't understand
That make me confused and
befuddled
So don't go to sleep
when you turn out the light
Cos sometimes I like to be
cuddled

squeeeze

← us having
a lovely
cuddle

Special Tip

Boyfriends can never get tired of being told how amazing they are

Other Girls

Never trust a boyfriend who says he doesn't fancy other girls...

...he's fibbing

a poem about
Man's Talk

Men think they can impress us
By saying they've broken girls'
hearts
If only they'd think with their
brains
Instead of their private parts

Special Tip for Girls

Boyfriends <u>really</u> do think tarty undies are smashing

...even if your girlfriends don't

a poem for
A Boyfriend

There's something I think I should
tell you
I hope you don't get a big head
You're not only gorgeously
handsome and cool
But you're totally brilliant in bed

a poem about
Sex Maniacs

They dream about sex every hour
of the day
They dream when they work
And they dream when they play
They dream about sex in the bath
and in bed
They never get naughty thoughts
out of their head

Warning :-

As soon as men start drinking there is only one thing on their minds

a poem about

Men

Men think they're amazing
But I'll tell you what I think
Their brains are in their willies
And they only fart and drink

Sneaky Tip

If you want to do something with your boyfriend - make him think it was his idea

Men always like to think they're right

Sport

Boyfriends waste at least half of their lives watching sport

a poem about a
Football Fan

Why do men talk about football
When most of them don't even
play?
They chant and they cheer
And swig loads of beer
And just watch it on telly all day

'ere we go 'ere we go

'ere we go

Annoying Things Boyfriends Do

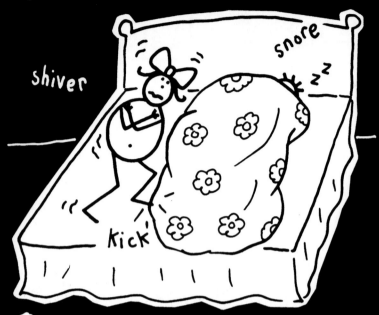

1. Hog the blankets

2. Forget your birthday

a poem about a
Perfect Man

Most girls want a man who is
                    perfect
But maybe not many exist
Who've got charm and panache
Several sackloads of cash
And a willy the size of your wrist

hi girls!

dosh

↑
manly bulge

FRIENDS

a poem about Good Friends

When you've got friends you
can talk to
You don't have to try to be clever
It's so much more fun
To sit down on your bum
And go through your love lives
together

a poem about
Friends

Some people think that it's great
to be rich
To be cool and keep up with the
trends
But riches and looks just don't
matter at all
Cos what really counts is your friends

no cash

smashing mates

Nev's latest tie

a shy poem
To Someone I Like

I sometimes find it rather hard
To say I really care
And that I like you quite a lot,
But I've said it now — so there

blush

shuffle

a poem about
Missing You

There are times when I really
do miss you

And think of you missing me too

So I close my eyes tight

And I daydream

That I am together with you

lovely
daydream

a poem about a
Huggle

A huggle is something you share
with a friend
You can huggle in all kinds of ways
Huggling makes you feel all sort
of warm
And perfectly splendid for days

us after
a good
huggle

a poem about

My Friend

A friend is a person who helps
you to laugh
And makes you feel happy and free
A friend is the grooviest thing
you can have
A friend is what you are to ME

us having a
smashing time

Fizz

gurgle

a poem called

↓

Thinking of You

I'm thinking of you lots and lots
So here's what I can do
I'm sending loads of happy vibes
And friendly thoughts to you

a poem about

My Little Plan

The fact that you're so smashing
Made me hatch a little plan
I wanted just to tell you

I'm your all-time greatest fan

a poem about a
Cuddle Token

I've got you something wonderful
That can't be smashed or broken
I hope you use it lots
'Cos it's my special Cuddle Token

a poem to say
↓

You Make Me Happy

Sometimes I close my eyes tightly
And dream of you while you're away
Cos thinking of you makes me happy
So that's what I wanted to say

a poem saying ↓ I Like You

You tell me I'm fat and I'm ugly
You tell me I'm utterly nuts
You tell me I burp and I fart and
                                    I smell
But that's why I like you so much

a poem to say
You're Special

You're a very special person
And you mean a lot to me
When you're around you make
the world
A better place to be

happy

a poem about

My Own Little Way

I sometimes get rather embarrassed
And don't always know what to say
When it comes to expressing my
                              feelings
But I try in my own little way

a lovely
Hugging Poem

I want you to know
That I think you are great
And although I'm a bit of a mug
If you ever need me
I'll always be near
To come round and give you a hug

squeeze

a poem about

Being Friends

If you need some cheering up
Because you're sad or blue
Or you need someone to talk to
I'll be always there for you

a
Friendly Poem

Never think twice about calling me up
To say that your pride has been dented
To tell me you're happy or lonely or sad
'Cos that is why friends were invented

a poem for a

Lovely Person

Has anyone recently told you
How totally lovely you are?
If not here's a poem to tell you
That this person thinks you're
a star

Hooray

LOVELIEST PERSON IN THE WHOLE WORLD EVER

a poem for

My Groovy Mate

Thanks for being so groovy
Thanks for being so great
Thanks for being so totally fab
Thanks for being my mate

a poem for an
Extra Special Person

If I had a million pounds
I know what I would do
I'd buy some extra special times
And spend them all with you